"Because technology such as software requires huge fixed investment up-front, but involves trivial marginal costs, it is highly likely that competition will result in 'fragile monopolies' being created, with single companies dominating segments for a time, until they are toppled by rivals." *The Economist*, "The New Enforcers." October 7, 2000.

I. INTRODUCTION

The ability of incumbent firms to maintain their market power by deterring entry has been a topic of considerable interest for some time. With the advent of game theory, economists have recognized that entry deterrence strategies must be credible. Imposing this credibility requirement on an incumbent's strategy in a price or quantity setting game with the entrant has had a profound effect on the analysis of several types of entry deterrence strategies, such as limit pricing (e.g., Milgrom and Roberts 1982) or capacity expansion (e.g., Dixit 1980). Typically, however, these analyses have not considered the credibility of the incumbent's decision to remain in the market or to exit. They have assumed parameter values such that exit is never optimal (the no exit threat is always credible) or that the incumbent can commit not to exit the market. In industries with large fixed, but not sunk, costs, however, exit can be the profit maximizing strategy when faced with an entrant who may be much more efficient or have a far superior product. American Airlines, for example, decided to abandon its San Jose hub and many routes within California shortly after Southwest Airlines entered the San Jose market (San Jose Mercury News 1993; Washington Post 1993). In fact, as the above quote indicates, the credibility of the no exit threat could become increasingly important as rapidly advancing technology provides opportunities for entrants to topple dominant firms in many industries. Thus, it is more important than ever to analyze the effect of the exit option on the ability of incumbents to deter entry.

1

This is especially true given that this paper shows that allowing for the possibility that the incumbent may want to exit the market (and, thus, requiring that the threat to remain in the market after entry be credible) can have as profound effects on entry deterrence strategies as does imposing the credibility constraint on the incumbent's pricing or output strategy. This is true both when the entry deterrence strategy in question is of the type that affects the entrant's perceptions about profitability given entry (e.g., limit pricing), and when they are of the type that actually do affect future profitability (e.g., investments in capacity expansion or cost reduction or advertising).

In the case of limit pricing, while one might think that the possibility of exit[1] always makes limit pricing less effective at deterring entry, this is not necessarily the case. In separating equilibria, of course, since the incumbent's type is perfectly revealed, the possibility of exit does not change the fact that limit pricing does not affect the entry probability. For pooling equilibria, however, introducing the possibility of exit does matter. In particular, when exit is allowed, the high cost incumbent is less likely to pool (in a partial pooling equilibrium[2]), i.e., choose the same first period price as a low cost incumbent, than if it could not exit (because, say, fixed costs were sunk). Not pooling, and thus inducing entry, is now more attractive to the incumbent because it isn't forced to remain in the market when this results in negative profits. This effect tends to make entry more likely when exit is possible.

---

[1] I will often speak of comparisons between cases where exit is possible and where it is not. This can be thought of as either comparing models where the incumbent can not commit not to exit to models where it can or as comparing models where levels of avoidable fixed costs are such that exit is sometimes optimal versus models where these costs are so small (almost all fixed costs are sunk) that it is never optimal.

[2] I define a partial pooling equilibrium as one where the high cost incumbent chooses the pooling action with positive probability less than one and separates with the complementary probability.

Because of this, however, the entrant is actually less likely to enter after observing the pooling price when exit is possible than when it isn't (because the entrant is more likely to be up against a low cost incumbent). This more than makes up for the fact that if it is up against a high cost incumbent, the entrant will earn monopoly rather than duopoly profits due to exit. The net effect, then, of allowing exit on the total probability of entry is ambiguous. I show, however, that which effect dominates depends on the cost of the high cost incumbent. In fact, when the high cost incumbent's costs are especially high, entry can actually be *less* probable when one allows for exit.

In the limit pricing model, I assume that while the incumbent's type is private information, the entrant's type is common knowledge. When analyzing the effect of exit on entry deterrence strategies that directly affect future profitability, I examine the reverse case: the incumbent's type is common knowledge while only the entrant knows its type. I do this to show how entry-deterring strategies can affect the credibility of the incumbent's threat to remain in the market after entry. The crucial insight here is somewhat similar to Nalebuff's (1987) insight about the effect of credibility in pretrial settlement negotiations. The more the incumbent invests in decreasing the profitability of entry, the stronger a competitor it is likely to face given that entry occurs. This reduces the credibility of the incumbent's threat not to exit.

In fact, I show that when exit is possible, but not inevitable, the *only* way the incumbent can deter entry is by making the no exit threat more credible; that is, by increasing its expected duopoly profits. Reducing the profitability of entry into a duopoly market will have no independent effect on the probability of entry. While investments in cost reduction still have entry deterring properties, it is only because they make the

3

profits of the incumbent, given entry, larger, not because they also reduce the profits of an entrant. Increases in the fixed cost of entry, however, have *no* effect on entry probability because they don't affect the incumbent's profits given entry, and thus don't affect its incentives to exit. Thus, strategies such as lobbying for tighter environmental standards for new plants will *not* be effective in deterring entry when exit is possible (but not certain). This will even be true for regulations that raise the marginal costs of a new entrant, thus reducing its expected profit from entry, so long as they also raise the incumbent's marginal cost enough to reduce its profitability in the event of entry. As surprising as this may seem, it follows because the higher the cost of entry or the less profitable duopoly competition is for the entrant, the more effective a competitor an entrant must be to warrant entry. This reduces the expected profits of the incumbent, making it more likely to exit. This increase in the exit probability then induces more entry, counteracting the increase in the entry cost.

On the other hand, advertising that expands the market for both the incumbent and the entrant can actually *deter* entry when exit is possible, even though it would encourage entry were exit not possible. Again, the reason is that by increasing the demand for the product, the incumbent increases its expected profits if entry occurs.[3] This makes it less likely it will exit, making entry less attractive. This effect more than compensates for the direct effect of the larger market on the profitability of entry.

While most of the literature on entry deterrence has assumed that exit by the incumbent firm is never optimal, there are a few exceptions. Judd (1985), in a model of

---

[3] One can imagine some types of demand curves (such as constant elasticity demand) where parallel shifts of the demand curve might actually reduce duopoly profits by inducing each firm to act compete more aggressively. In these unusual circumstances, advertising that induced such a parallel shift in the demand curve would not deter entry since it would not increase the incumbent's duopoly profits. I thank Jeremy Bulow for pointing this out.

spatial competition, shows that, when the incumbent can exit, its ability to pre-empt entry into a nearby product by entering first is limited. Eaton and Lipsey (1980) allow for exit to discuss the optimal durability and replacement of sunk capital. Neither of these papers, however, considers the impact of exit on the type of entry deterrence strategies discussed here.[4] Moreover, both use complete information models, so the interaction of asymmetric information and exit, which is the essence of this paper, is not present in either of those papers.

In the limit pricing literature, LeBlanc (1992) allows the incumbent firm to exit and recover some of its fixed costs. Thus, his model contains some exit in some equilibria. His focus, however, is not on the effect of exit on the effectiveness of limit pricing. In fact, since he only examines separating equilibria, and pooling equilibria are the only ones where exit affects the ability of limit pricing to deter entry, he does not derive any results about the role of exit in limit pricing strategies.

In the investment in entry deterrence literature, both Arvan (1986) and Bagwell and Ramey (1996) (in capacity models) allow for the possibility of exit by the incumbent following entry. In Arvan's paper, however, the only uncertainty is about the incumbent's technology, not the entrant's. So the effect I describe about the interaction of the entry deterring strategy with the credibility of the no exit threat does not exist in Arvan's paper. In Bagwell and Ramey there is no asymmetric information, but they do derive a link between capacity expansion and exit by assuming forward induction. This,

---

[4] The spatial preemption model of Judd (1985) could be seen as a special case of the strategies I discuss in Section III. However, since there is no uncertainty in his model and the entry deterrence strategy is of fixed magnitude, the equilibrium result is exit with probability one. Therefore, the most interesting equilibrium in Section III, the mixed strategy equilibrium, doesn't arise in Judd's model. By the same token, since this paper doesn't consider spatial markets, the model in Section III doesn't cover the interesting aspects of Judd's model. Thus, while his paper has similarities with this one, the situations it covers and its results are quite distinct.

essentially, gives the entrant a limited ability to commit to its output level. The way this works is that, under forward induction, the incumbent assumes that the entrant will produce a large enough quantity to cover its entry costs assuming the incumbent takes this output level as given. A consequence of giving the entrant this commitment ability is that the incumbent then wants to constrain its capacity so that the entrant can enter and make positive profit without the incumbent exiting. Like their paper, I also show that exit can make entry deterrence strategies less effective. My paper, however, gets this result by introducing asymmetric information rather than limited entrant commitment made possible by assuming forward induction. This distinction is fundamental because it is both the possibility of exit and uncertainty about the entrant's type that generate the result that entry deterrence is accomplished solely by decreasing the incentive to exit, not by decreasing the profitability of entry.

The plan of the paper is as follows. In Section II, I discuss the effect of exit on strategies, such as limit pricing, that only affect the entrant's perceptions about the profitability of entry. Section III discusses entry deterrence strategies that affect the actual profitability of entry. Section IV concludes. The Appendix contains the proof of the first and third propositions.

II. STRATEGIES THAT AFFECT PERCEPTIONS: LIMIT PRICING

To show how the possibility of exit changes the effectiveness of limit pricing, I consider a simple model where there are fixed, but not sunk, costs of operating in any period. These costs, which can differ between the entrant and the incumbent, are common knowledge. The entrant's marginal cost is also common knowledge, but the incumbent's marginal cost is private information. The set up of the game is as follows.

In period 1, only the incumbent, I, is in the market. It chooses some action, $a \in A$, that affects its profits in period 1 but has no effect on its profits, or the entrant's, in period 2 *conditional* on the market structure that exists in period 2. The potential entrant, E, observes a. Period 2 is divided into three stages. In period 2.1, the entrant decides whether or not to enter the market. In period 2.2, the incumbent, having observed the entry decision, decides whether or not to exit the market. In period 2.3, the incumbent and entrant (if in the market) earn profits, which vary according to the entry and exit decisions. The following timeline depicts the sequence of events.

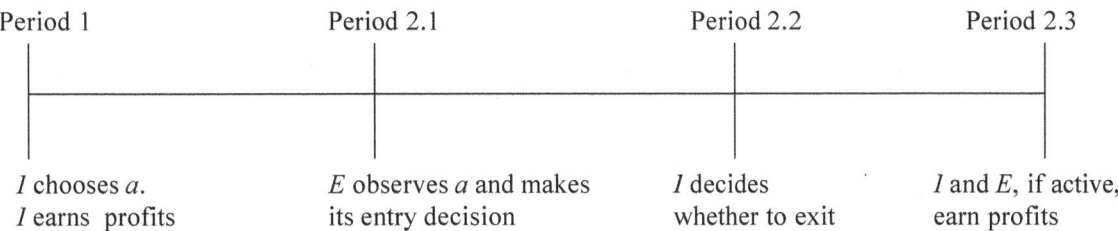

Period 1	Period 2.1	Period 2.2	Period 2.3
I chooses a. I earns profits	E observes a and makes its entry decision	I decides whether to exit	I and E, if active, earn profits

Notice that while I have allowed the incumbent to save avoidable fixed costs by exiting the market after observing the entrant's entry decision, I do not allow the entrant to exit, and save its entry costs, after observing the incumbent's exit decision. This is the essence of the difference between the model in this paper and prior models of limit pricing. If the entrant could back out of its entry decision at zero cost, the initial entry decision would be meaningless. Thus, the model would be identical to those where the incumbent can commit to remaining in the market even after the observing entry behavior. Relaxing this assumption is the essence of the paper.

One might think that the timing assumption is still peculiar in that, after the entrant pays a sunk entry cost, the incumbent and entrant are still not on equal footing. The incumbent has the option to exit, saving some avoidable fixed costs, while the entrant does not. This assumption, however, is not essential. If I modified period 2.2 to allow the incumbent and the entrant to make simultaneous exit decisions (and divided up the entry costs into a sunk portion, paid in 2.1, and an avoidable portion, paid in 2.3) the equilibrium of the old game is still an equilibrium of the new game. If the incumbent thinks that after the entrant sinks its entry costs in period 2.1 it will never exit in period 2.2, its exit strategy in 2.2 will be unchanged. Thus, anytime the entrant wants to enter in the original game it will enter in the modified game and not exit. So, as long as there is an equilibrium of the game outlined in the above figure where the entrant enters, the same equilibrium will obtain in this modified game.[5]

Thus, the incumbent's inter-temporal profit function can be written as follows:

(1)
$$\Pi_I(a,c) = \pi_{I1}(a,c) - f +$$
$$\beta\{p_e(a)(1 - p_x(a,c))(\pi_{I2d}(c) - f) + (1 - p_e(a))(\pi_{I2m}(c) - f)\}$$

In each period that the incumbent operates, it incurs an avoidable fixed cost, f. This cost is avoidable in that if it exits the market, it doesn't pay f. In period 1, the firm's gross profit is a function of its action, a (in the limit pricing interpretation a is the first period price), and its marginal cost parameter, c, (which only I knows). Profits in period 2, discounted by β, depend on the entry and exit decisions. With probability $p_e(a)$ E enters. If that happens, I will exit with probability $p_x(a,c)$. If I exits, it earns zero profits. If E enters and I does not exit, I earns the period 2 gross duopoly profit level $\pi_{I2d}(c)$. If E does not enter, then I earns the period 2 gross monopoly profit level $\pi_{I2m}(c)$. I assume

---

[5] There could be another equilibrium (at least for some parameter values) of this modified game where a high cost incumbent does not exit in period 2.2 with positive probability, inducing the entrant to exit in period 2.2, which means the entrant will never enter in period 2.1. Not only will this alternate equilibrium not exist for all parameter values, unlike the equilibrium described in the text, the alternate equilibrium is inconsistent with forward induction (see Bagwell and Ramey 1996): In period 2.2 if a high cost incumbent observes entry it will have to assume the entrant will not exit or else the entrant would have been better off not entering in 2.1.

that $\pi_{I2m}(c) > f$, so that when E does not enter, I never exits. Given its cost parameter, c, I chooses a to maximize (1).

From here on, I will examine the simple case where there are just two possible cost parameters for I, $c_H > c_L$. The ex ante probability that I's cost parameter is c_H is q. E's cost parameter, known to all, is c_E. E's expected period 2 profits from entry are as follows:

$$\begin{aligned} (2) \quad \pi_E(a) &= p_H(a)[(1 - p_x(a,c_H))\pi_{E2dH} + p_x(a,c_H)\pi_{E2m}] \\ &+ (1 - p_H(a))[(1 - p_x(a,c_L))\pi_{E2dL} + p_x(a,c_L)\pi_{E2m}] - f_E \end{aligned}$$

With probability $p_H(a)$, I has high costs (notice that this is the posterior probability that the incumbent has high costs given the action observed in period 1). Given that, if I does not exit, then E earns gross duopoly profits π_{E2dH}. If I does exit, then E earns gross monopoly profits of π_{E2m}. With probability $(1 - p_H(a))$, I has low costs. In this case, I's exit probability and E's duopoly profits are adjusted accordingly. To enter the market, E must pay the fixed cost f_E.

Because I want to examine the perfect Bayesian equilibrium of this model, I require that $p_H(a)$ be determined in accordance with Bayes' rule. That is:

$$(3) \qquad\qquad p_H(a) = \frac{qL_H(a)}{qL_H(a) + (1-q)L_L(a)}$$

In (3), L_i represents the likelihood that an incumbent with cost level c_i would choose action a.

In this simple model, exit only matters if the high cost incumbent will exit if the entrant enters and the low cost incumbent will not. Thus, I assume that $\pi_{I2d}(c_H) < f < \pi_{I2d}(c_L)$. It is well known that in models of this type both pooling and separating equilibria are possible. In separating equilibria, the incumbent's type is perfectly revealed, so limit pricing never deters entry whether exit is possible or not. Thus, the effect of exit on separating equilibria is not very interesting. I will confine the analysis to equilibria with at least some pooling. That is, if a_P is the (pooling) action chosen by the low cost incumbent, a high cost incumbent chooses a_P with positive probability. For this to be a perfect Bayesian equilibrium the following conditions must hold:

(4a) $$\pi_E(a_P) \leq 0$$

(4b) $$\Pi_I(a_P, c_i) \geq \Pi_I(a, c_i) \, \forall a \in A, i = L, H$$

Condition (4a) requires that in any pooling equilibrium entry must be deterred with positive probability. If this condition doesn't hold, then entry is inevitable and thus both types of incumbents should choose the myopically optimal a, which I assume differs across types. Condition (4b) is just the condition that the pooling equilibrium action, a_P, is weakly optimal (given the beliefs of the entrant) for both types of incumbents. Given the assumption about the duopoly profit functions of the high and low cost incumbent, condition (4a) can be written as follows:

(4a?) $$p_H(a_P)\pi_{E2m} + (1 - p_H(a_P))\pi_{E2dL} - f_E \leq 0$$

Notice that if (4a?) holds for $p_H(a_P) = q$ (the posterior probability that an incumbent has high costs equals the prior probability), then there exists a complete pooling equilibrium (a pooling equilibrium where the high cost incumbent chooses a_P with probability 1). If (4a?) holds strictly for $p_H(a_P) = q$, then entry and exit never occur in the pooling equilibrium, so exit does not affect this pooling equilibrium. If (4a?) holds at equality for $p_H(a_P) = q$, then there will be a complete pooling equilibrium with the incumbent

10

choosing action a_P both if exit is possible and if it isn't. Because the entrant is indifferent about entry when there is exit, however, the exit pooling equilibrium (unlike the same equilibrium when exit is precluded) will involve entry, exit, and duopoly with positive probability. Below, I consider what happens when (4a?) does not hold for $p_H(a_P) = q$, so a complete pooling equilibrium is impossible.

When complete pooling is impossible, the high cost incumbent must be indifferent between mimicking the low cost incumbent and choosing its myopically optimal a, a_H. Thus, the high cost incumbent plays the mixed strategy of choosing a_P with probability r_p and a_H with probability $1 - r_p$. Then, r_p must be small enough so that (4a?) holds when $p_H(a_P)$ is given by (3). The following proposition compares incomplete pooling equilibria in this model to similar equilibria when the incumbent can commit not to exit.[6]

Proposition 1. Assume a complete pooling equilibrium does not exist. Consider any partial pooling equilibrium with the pooling action a_P. (a) There is less pooling with exit, that is, the high cost incumbent chooses a_P with strictly lower probability when exit is an option than when it is not. (b) If a_P is not a complete pooling equilibrium when exit is impossible, then, conditional on observing the pooling action, a_P, the entrant enters less often when exit is an option than when it is not. (c) If a_P is not a complete pooling equilibrium when exit is impossible, then, unconditionally, entry occurs with greater

---

[6]The comparison in this proposition between the exit case and the no exit case is NOT equivalent to a comparison of pooling equilibria where a high cost incumbent's duopoly profits are zero and when they are negative. While it is true that introducing the possibility of exit changes the high cost incumbent's duopoly profit in the second period from some negative amount to zero, it has an additional effect. That is, when the high cost incumbent can exit, this also increases the entrant's profit from entry when she is facing a high cost incumbent. Hence, this proposition is not simply a special case of the standard limit pricing results.

probability when exit is an option if and only if $c_H < c_H{}^*$. $c_H{}^*$ is implicitly defined by

the equation

$$(\pi_{E2d}(c_H{}^*) - \pi_{E2d}(c_L))(\pi_{E2m} - f_E)(\pi_{12m}(c_H{}^*) - f) =$$
$$(\pi_{E2d}(c_H{}^*) - f_E)(\pi_{E2m} - \pi_{E2d}(c_L))(\pi_{12m}(c_H{}^*) - \pi_{12d}(c_H{}^*))$$

if a_P completely deters entry in the exit case. If a_P does not completely deter entry in the

exit case then $c_H{}^*$ is implicitly defined by the equation

$$(\pi_{E2d}(c_H{}^*) - \pi_{E2d}(c_L))(\pi_{E2m} - f_E)(f - \pi_{12d}(c_H{}^*)) =$$
$$(f_E - \pi_{E2d}(c_L))(\pi_{E2m} - \pi_{E2d}(c_H{}^*))(\pi_{12m}(c_H{}^*) - \pi_{12d}(c_H{}^*))$$

Proof. See Appendix.

At first glance, Proposition 1 (especially part (b)) may seem somewhat counter-intuitive: the entrant enters less often (with smaller probability) after observing the pooling action a_P when the incumbent can exit than when it can't. This is explained as follows. Because a_P represents a partial pooling equilibrium, the high cost incumbent is indifferent between it and choosing its myopically optimal action a_H. Also, because a_P is a pooling equilibrium, the entrant must make non-positive profits (when exit is possible) if it enters after observing a_P. Now, suppose exit is not possible. A high cost incumbent will find the separating action, a_H, strictly less profitable than it did when it could exit, since it now must earn negative profits after entry. To restore indifference, the pooling action, a_P must be less profitable also. This requires that the entrant enter with a larger probability when exit is impossible (hence, with a smaller probability when exit is possible) after observing a_P. Similarly, now that the high cost incumbent does not exit after entry, the entrant earns a strictly lower profit from entry when exit is impossible, making no entry strictly preferable. To make entry more profitable, restoring the

12

entrant's indifference, it must face high cost incumbent with greater probability after observing the pooling action. Thus, the high cost incumbent must pool more often when exit is impossible (or less often when exit is possible).

The comparison of the total amount of entry, then, depends on the strength of the two competing effects. With exit, a high cost incumbent tries to deter entry by pooling less often, but pooling is more successful at deterring entry. When a high cost incumbent's costs are very high, the second effect dominates; there is less entry when exit is possible. Otherwise, there is more total entry when the incumbent can exit after observing entry than when it can't. The reason for this is that the exit option is relatively more valuable to the high cost incumbent the higher its costs are (the higher its costs the more negative its profits are after entry if it cannot exit). Thus, the amount by which a_H is more profitable when exit is possible relative to when it isn't is increasing in the high cost incumbent's costs. So, to maintain indifference, the amount by which the probability of entry falls (when exit is possible relative to when it isn't), again, given the pooling action, must be greater the higher the high cost incumbent's costs.

To see that it is possible to have either more or less entry when exit is possible, consider two extreme values for c_H. First, if c_H is very large, then the entrant's profit in duopoly will only be marginally lower than its monopoly profit. Thus, the fraction of high cost incumbents that choose the pooling action need only be marginally higher when exit is not possible to ensure that the entrant remains indifferent about entry when exit is not possible. When the high cost incumbent cannot exit, however, choosing a_H becomes much less profitable because its losses after entry are much larger due to its very high costs. Thus, to ensure that a_P is not more profitable than a_H now that exit is not possible,

13

the probability of entry, conditional on a_P, must be much larger when exit is not possible. So, when exit is not possible and c_H is very large a high cost incumbent chooses the pooling (entry-deterring) action with only a marginally larger probability as when exit is possible, but that action is much less effective at deterring entry. So there will be, on balance, more entry when exit is impossible than when it is possible.

On the other hand, if c_H is small enough that the high cost incumbent is only barely better of by exiting after entry, then the myopically optimal action, a_H, is only slightly better for it when exit is possible than when it isn't. As a result, the entry will have to occur only slightly more often (given the pooling action) when exit is impossible compared to when it is possible. High cost incumbents, however, will still need to choose the pooling action with a much larger probability when exit is not possible to ensure that the ex post probability that an entrant is facing a high cost incumbent is large enough so that the entrant still makes zero expected profits from entry even though it will only earn duopoly profits. In this case, then, the probability of entry conditional on pooling is only marginally larger (when exit is not possible) while the probability of pooling itself (which is the action that can deter entry) is much larger when exit is impossible. So, on balance, when c_H is very small, entry is less probable when exit is not possible than when it is.

Of course, the proposition doesn't say anything about separating equilibria. From Milgrom and Roberts (1982), however, we already know that in separating equilibria limit pricing is completely ineffective at deterring entry. Thus, in analyzing the effectiveness of limit pricing strategies, pooling equilibria are the important ones to focus on. For those equilibria, the message of Proposition 1 is that assuming incumbents can't exit the market is not a benign assumption when judging the effectiveness of limit pricing strategies. When the pooling equilibrium is complete, the possibility of exit unambiguously reduces the effectiveness of limit pricing at deterring entry. When the pooling equilibrium is incomplete, the option to exit will limit the effectiveness of deterring entry if the high cost incumbent's costs are not too high. Otherwise, the option to exit will actually increase the effectiveness of this entry deterrence strategy.

III. STRATEGIES THAT AFFECT FUTURE PROFITABILITY

In this section, I examine the effect of exit on entry deterrence strategies that operate by affecting actual future profitability rather than the entrant's perceptions of the profitability of entry. In order to make the distinction clean, in this section the entrant will have the private information, not the incumbent. Therefore, any entry deterrence strategy by the incumbent will not influence the entrant's perception of the incumbent's type. Entry deterrence can only work by affecting the actual profitability in period 2. The types of strategies I have in mind here are incumbent investment in cost reduction (or capacity expansion) in period 1 that has the effect of reducing the incumbent's marginal cost in period 2 or advertising by the incumbent in period 1 that affects the demand for the product in period 2. The incumbent could also sign exclusive contracts with suppliers (or buy up critical resources that are in limited supply) that increase either the marginal or the fixed cost of the entrant in period 2 (notice that some of these strategies will affect the entrant's profits even if the incumbent exits).

The model in this section differs from the model in Section II in the following ways. First, the incumbent's marginal cost parameter, c, is common knowledge. Second, the entrant's marginal cost parameter, c_E, is private information to the entrant. The incumbent knows only that it is distributed according to the cumulative distribution function G, with associated density function g, with support $[c_E, \overline{c_E}]$. In period 1, the incumbent takes an action, $a \in A$, that affects both its profits in period 1 and (potentially) its own profits and the profits of the potential entrant (should it enter) in period 2. The potential entrant, E, observes a. Period 2 proceeds exactly as in Section II. For this model, c and c_E could also be interpreted as parameters measuring the quality of the goods rather than their production cost. For this interpretation, higher c and c_E should be thought of as lower quality. I employ the Bayesian Nash equilibrium concept for this game.

Because the entrant's costs are private information, the incumbent's response to entry cannot be conditioned on the entrant's type. The entrant's profits from entry are:

(5) $$\pi_E(a, c_E) = (1 - p_x(a))\pi_{E2d}(a, c_E) + p_x(a)\pi_{E2m}(a, c_E) - f_E$$

Notice that this is strictly decreasing in its marginal cost parameter, c_E. I assume that the support for c_E is such that, for any a the incumbent might choose, there exists a cutoff level for the entrant's cost parameter $\hat{c}_E(a) \in [c_E, \overline{c_E}]$ such that if the entrant's cost are $\hat{c}_E(a)$ it makes exactly zero profits from entry. Thus, if the entrant has a smaller cost parameter than this cutoff value, $c_E < \hat{c}_E(a)$, the entrant enters, otherwise it does not. Of course, the exact value of $\hat{c}_E(a)$ will depend on the exit strategy of the incumbent, but, as I show below, this will also be determined by a, its period 1 action. In the figure below, the incumbent can move the cutoff line at $\hat{c}_E(a)$ to the left by its choice of a.

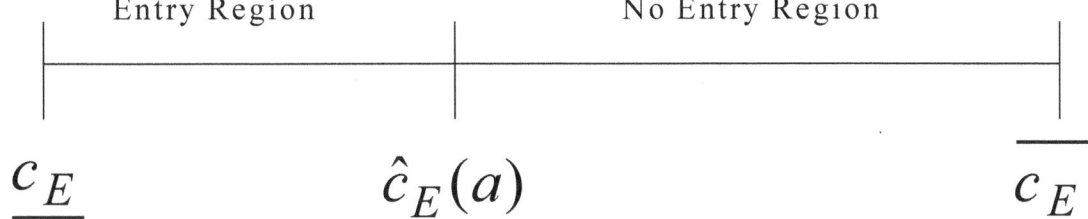

Given this entry strategy, the incumbent's inter-temporal profit function can be written as follows:

$$\Pi_I(a) = \pi_{I1}(a) - f +$$

$$(6) \quad \beta\{(1 - p_x(a))\int_{\underline{c}_E}^{\hat{c}_E(a)}(\pi_{I2d}(a,c_E) - f)g(c_E)dc_E + (1 - G(\hat{c}_E(a)))(\pi_{I2m}(a) - f)\}$$

In period 1, the incumbent is a monopolist and earns the associated profit, $\pi_{I1}(a)$, less its fixed operating cost of f. This profit is a function of a in that the monopolist's first period profit will be reduced if it invests in second period cost reduction or advertising to increase second period demand. Thus, I will think of $\pi'_{I1}(a)$ as being negative. Its second period profits are discounted by ß. When the entrant enters, which happens when its costs are between $[\underline{c}_E, \hat{c}_E(a))$, if the incumbent exits it earns zero. If the incumbent doesn't exit, which happens with probability $(1 - p_x(a))$, the incumbent pays its fixed cost f and earns gross duopoly profits of $\pi_{I2d}(a,c_E)$. These are increasing in c_E, and I will often assume they are increasing in a (though they need not always be, depending on the type of action the incumbent takes), as they would be if a is cost reduction investment or advertising. If the entrant's costs are high enough that it doesn't enter, the incumbent earns monopoly profits in period 2, again generally (though not always) increasing in a, and pays its fixed cost f.

There can be equilibria where the incumbent always exits upon entry. For example, consider an entrant of type $c_{E1}(a)$ such that it earns zero profits as a monopolist, that is, $\pi_{E2m}(a, c_{E1}(a)) - f_E = 0$. If $\int_{\underline{c_E}}^{c_{E1}(a)} (\pi_{12d}(a, c_E) - f) g(c_E) dc_E \leq 0$ then the incumbent's expected profits are non-positive if it does not exit. Hence, it will always exit if the entrant enters, and all entrants with $c_E < c_{E1}(a)$ enter. In such cases, however, a can still have value to the incumbent since it may reduce the probability of entry and may increase the incumbent's profits in period 2.3 when there is no entry. I define the set A_1 as follows:

$$A_1 = \{a \in A : \pi_{E2m}(a, c_{E1}(a)) - f_E = 0, \int_{\underline{c_E}}^{c_{E1}(a)} (\pi_{12d}(a, c_E) - f) g(c_E) dc_E \leq 0\}$$

If $a \in A_1$ then the incumbent exits with probability one if there is entry.

It is also possible for the incumbent to never want to exit upon entry. Consider $c_{E2}(a)$ such that $\pi_{E2d}(a, c_{E2}(a)) - f_E = 0$. If $\int_{\underline{c_E}}^{c_{E2}(a)} (\pi_{12d}(a, c_E) - f) g(c_E) dc_E > 0$ then all entrants with $c_E < c_{E2}(a)$ enter, and the incumbent never exits.[7] If it is optimal for the incumbent to choose a such that this equilibrium obtains, then the option to exit makes no difference. I define the set A_2 as follows:

$$A_2 = \{a \in A : \pi_{E2d}(a, c_{E2}(a)) - f_E = 0, \int_{\underline{c_E}}^{c_{E2}(a)} (\pi_{12d}(a, c_E) - f) g(c_E) dc_E > 0\}$$

---

[7] Even in this case, however, there could be equilibria where the incumbent exits with positive probability and entrants with higher costs than $c_{E2}(a)$ enter. If so, the analysis that follows will apply to these equilibria as well.

The set A_2 is the set of all actions that for which there is an equilibrium where the incumbent does not exit in period 2.2. Thus, if $a \notin A_1 \cup A_2$ then the incumbent will exit with some probability $p_x(a) \in (0,1)$. The following analysis is for this case.

Since $p_x(a) \in (0,1)$, the incumbent must earn zero profits when it remains in the market after exit. That is, the entrant's entry strategy, to enter if its costs are less than $\hat{c}_E(a)$, must be such that:

(7)
$$\int_{\underline{c}_E}^{\hat{c}_E(a)} (\pi_{12d}(a,c_E) - f)g(c_E)dc_E = 0$$

Equation (7) implicitly defines the entry cutoff $\hat{c}_E(a)$. Given this cutoff, the probability that the incumbent exits after entry is determined to ensure that the entrant whose costs are $\hat{c}_E(a)$ breaks even by entering:

(8)
$$(1 - p_x(a))\pi_{E2d}(a,\hat{c}_E(a)) + p_x(a)\pi_{E2m}(a,\hat{c}_E(a)) - f_E = 0$$

Thus, the probability of exit is the following:

(9)
$$p_x(a) = \frac{\pi_{E2d}(a,\hat{c}_E(a)) - f_E}{\pi_{E2d}(a,\hat{c}_E(a)) - \pi_{E2m}(a,\hat{c}_E(a))}$$

By differentiating (7) with respect to a, one can see how entry cutoff varies with a; that is, how effective an action a is at deterring entry. Doing so gives the following:

(10)
$$\hat{c}'_E(a) = -\frac{\int_{\underline{c}_E}^{\hat{c}_E(a)} \frac{\partial(\pi_{12d}(a,c_E) - f)}{\partial a}g(c_E)dc_E}{g(\hat{c}_E(a))(\pi_{12d}(a,\hat{c}_E(a)) - f)}$$

As (10) shows, increasing a (when $a \notin A_1 \cup A_2$) reduces entry if and only if increasing a increases the incumbent's gross duopoly profit. This follows because if the incumbent is to break even in expectation when the entrant enters, it must make positive net profits when the entrant is of the highest possible cost type. That is, $\pi_{12d}(a,\hat{c}_E(a)) - f > 0$.

By contrast, if exit is not possible, the cutoff level for entry, which I'll call $\hat{c}_{En}(a)$, will be determined implicitly by the following equation:

(11) $$\pi_{E2d}(a, \hat{c}_{En}(a)) - f_E = 0$$

Differentiating this with respect to a and solving for the effect of a on entry gives the following:

(12) $$\hat{c}'_{En}(a) = -\frac{d(\pi_{E2d}(a, \hat{c}_{En}(a)) - f_E)}{da} \Bigg/ \frac{d\pi_{E2d}(a, \hat{c}_{En}(a))}{dc_E}$$

Since the denominator is negative (increasing its cost parameter reduces the entrant's profits), when exit is not possible increasing a decreases the cutoff level for entry if and only if increasing a decreases the entrant's profits. Thus, I have proved the following proposition.

Proposition 2. For all $a \notin A_1 \cup A_2$, when exit is possible, a deters entry if and only if it increases the incumbent's duopoly profit, whereas, when exit is not possible, a deters entry if and only if it reduces the entrant's duopoly profit.

This distinction made by Proposition 2 is quite fundamental. When exit is possible, unless entry deterrence is either very cheap and avoidable fixed costs are large, or entry deterrence is very expensive and avoidable fixed costs are small, its effectiveness depends only on how it affects the incumbent's profits, not the entrant's.

So long as, for the set of entrants who find it profitable to enter as a duopolist, the incumbent does not want to exit, decreasing the entrant's profits from entry will decrease the cutoff value of the cost parameter, $\hat{c}_E(a)$, reducing the probability of entry. This is when $a \in A_2$. However, as the profitability of entry falls, it is only the more efficient

entrants who can profitably enter. This reduces the incumbent's profits in period 2.3.

Once the profitability of entry is reduced to the point where the incumbent earns

zero expected net profits from competing against the entrant, reducing the profitability of

entry, conditional on market structure, no longer deters entry (over the region

$a \notin A_1 \cup A_2$). The reason is that if the cutoff level of the cost parameter for entry

continues to fall, the incumbent will expect negative profits in period 2.3, so it will exit

with probability one. Knowing this, however, less efficient entrants (those with cost

parameters above $\hat{c}_E(a)$) will enter, which will induce the incumbent to remain in the

market. Thus, past the point where the incumbent earns zero expected profits in period

2.3, reducing the profitability of entry will only increase the incumbent's probability of

exit so as to continue to ensure that entrants with a cost parameter of $\hat{c}_E(a)$ break even

from entry. Of course, once the profitability of entry falls below the point where an

entrant with the old break even cost parameter $\hat{c}_E(a)$ can break even as a monopolist,

then decreasing the profitability of entry will again reduce the probability of entry and the

incumbent will exit whenever there is entry (now, $a \in A_1$).

On the other hand, if the incumbent's action increases its duopoly profits given

the efficiency of its competitor, it will remain indifferent about whether or not to exit

only if the expected efficiency of the entrant it faces has increased. Thus, the entry rule

must change (when $a \notin A_1 \cup A_2$) to have entry only when the entrant's cost parameter is

below some lower level than before. To ensure that a less efficient entrant does not want

to enter (since its profitability, conditional on the market structure, has not changed), the incumbent must exit with a smaller probability than if had not taken this action to improve its profitability.

Investments in marginal cost reduction (or quality enhancement) are entry-deterring strategies in both cases, though their effectiveness may differ greatly. Similarly, raising the entrant's marginal costs (or reducing its quality) are effective entry-deterring strategies with or without exit. Strategies that affect fixed costs, however, will operate quite differently in the two situations. When exit is possible, fixed costs of entry are not entry barriers, that is, they don't affect the probability of entry (so long as they aren't too high). Thus, increasing the entrant's fixed entry cost is pointless for the incumbent. As explained above, all that will do is increase the equilibrium exit probability without affecting the entry probability. On the other hand, if the incumbent can pay some of its fixed costs of operating before the entrant makes its entry decision (say by signing long-term employment contracts or long-term leases), this will deter entry by making its threat to remain in the market more credible. (Of course, to the extent these contracts could be renegotiated, the effectiveness of these strategies may be limited.)

This distinction also is critical when one considers the operation of advertising as an entry barrier. If the goods of the incumbent and the entrant are not highly differentiated, one might think that the incumbent would want to refrain from advertising to increase the size of the market because that might induce entry. When exit is possible, however, the exact opposite is the case. The incumbent will want to advertise to increase the size of the market, not only because doing so increases its profit the period 2, but also because it will deter entry. In this case, entry deterrence occurs because advertising has

22

made the incumbent's threat to remain in the market more credible. A similar argument would apply to investments in quality enhancement that are non-rival (improve the entrant's quality as much as the incumbent's). This effect is similar to Nalebuff's (1987) point about the importance of credibility in pretrial settlement negotiations.

One might wonder how sensitive the results in Proposition 2 are to the need for a mixed strategy equilibrium in this model. To shed some light on this question, consider tweaking the model as follows. Instead of the incumbent's cost parameter being common knowledge, assume that the incumbent is subject to some small, mean zero, cost shock in between period 1 and period 2. Then, instead of an incumbent being indifferent as to whether or not to exit in period 2.2, if the incumbent gets a favorable cost shock (say $s < s^*$) it remains in the market, otherwise it exits.[8]

Consider the effect of an action, a, that only reduces the profitability of entry. There must be some small effect on the entry cutoff level. If not, then an incumbent will still remain in the market if and only if $s < s^*$ (since the incumbent's expected profit from competing with the same distribution of possible entrants has not changed). So, an entrant whose cost parameter is exactly at the old cutoff level will not longer break even. As a result, the cutoff level for entry must fall, and this will reduce s^*. Since s^* falls, however, the probability that a potential entrant will be a monopolist increases. Thus, the cutoff level for entry cannot fall as much as it would if there were no exit. That is, the possibility of exit still reduces the ability of profit reducing strategies to deter entry, though it doesn't entirely eliminate their effectiveness.

As the magnitude of the cost uncertainty goes to zero, however, the effectiveness of reducing the profitability of entry does approach zero. If the possible cost parameters

---

[8] I thank Ezra Friedman for suggesting this case.

of the incumbent in period 2 are very tightly clustered then it only takes a very small reduction in the cutoff level of entry to cause a big shift in the probability of exit. Thus, the entrant must only be slightly more efficient to still break even after the incumbent has acted to reduce the entrant's profits. Thus, while stark nature of the results in Proposition 2 is dependent on the mixed strategy equilibrium, the results do not change in a knife-edge way when some uncertainty is introduced.

In addition, introducing this uncertainty will not change the fact that actions that only increase the duopoly profit of the incumbent deter entry. (By increasing s^*, they reduce the probability that the entrant will be a monopolist.) Whether or not a strategy, such as advertising, that increases profitability for both the incumbent and the entrant deters entry will depend on the magnitude of the uncertainty. The smaller the uncertainty about the incumbent's costs the more likely advertising will deter entry rather than encourage it.

Notice that when the conditions of Proposition 2 hold, there will necessarily be more entry when exit is possible than when it isn't. This follows because the condition for the entry cutoff when there is no exit, equation (11), says that all entrant types that can make non-negative duopoly profits, net of their fixed entry cost, enter. When exit is possible, however, equation (8) indicates the entrant's profits from entry are a weighted average of duopoly and monopoly profits. Since monopoly profits exceed duopoly profits, higher cost entrants will enter when exit is possible. If the conditions of Proposition 2 do not hold, there will either be exit whenever there is entry, in which case there is even more entry, or there will never be exit, in which case entry is unaffected by the exit option. Thus, not surprisingly, for entry deterrence strategies that actually affect future profitability, the exit option reduces the ability of incumbent to deter entry.

This does not necessarily imply, however, that the incumbent will make less effort to deter entry when exit is possible than it would were it impossible (where more effort is defined as a greater level of a, and thus more first period profits foregone). In fact, there is no clean comparison of the incumbent's incentives to forego profits to deter entry in the two cases because the entry deterrence mechanism is so different when exit is possible than when it isn't. This can be seen by examining the first order conditions for the entry deterrence action, a, in the two cases. When exit is possible (and occurs with positive probability) the marginal profit from a is the following:

$$(13) \quad \Pi'_I(a) = \pi'_{I1}(a) + \beta\{(1 - G(\hat{c}_E(a)))\pi'_{I2m}(a) - \hat{c}'_E(a)g(\hat{c}_E(a)))(\pi_{I2m}(a) - f)\}$$

This follows from differentiating (6) with respect to a, while fixing the incumbent's profit when there is entry at zero. By substituting in for $\hat{c}'_E(a)$ using equation (10), this becomes:

$$\Pi'_I(a) = \pi'_{I1}(a) +$$

$$(14) \quad \beta\{(1 - G(\hat{c}_E(a)))\pi'_{I2m}(a) + \frac{\pi_{I2m}(a) - f}{\pi_{I2d}(a, \hat{c}_E(a)) - f} \int_{\underline{c}_E}^{\hat{c}_E(a)} (d\pi_{I2d}(a, c_E)/da)g(c_E)dc_E\}$$

For simplicity, I have assumed in (13) and (14) (and (15) below) that a does not affect fixed costs, though this is not essential for this point. As (14) indicates, a increases second period profits in two ways. First, when the entrant won't enter anyway, it increases monopoly profits. Second, when the entrant would have entered, a increases duopoly profits. That is valuable, however, not because of the added profits given entry (that has to remain at zero to maintain the equilibrium), but, rather, because by reducing the incumbent's incentive to exit, it deters entry. From (14), one can see that the entry

25

deterrence value from a is strictly greater than the amount by which it increases duopoly

profits $(\dfrac{\pi_{12m}(a)-f}{\pi_{12d}(a,\hat{c}_E(a))-f}>1$, since monopoly is more profitable than duopoly). Thus,

when exit is possible, the incumbent will choose a strictly larger a than it would have

chosen if the only reason to choose a was to increase the incumbent's second period

profits, even if the incumbent could not exit and, thus, benefited from a with probability

one in period 2.

Notice, however, that the marginal profit from a, when exit is possible, is

independent of its effect on the entrant's profit. This is very different from the

incumbent's marginal benefit from a when exit is impossible. To see this, differentiate

(6) setting $p_x(a) = 0$:

$$\Pi'_I(a) = \pi'_{I1}(a) + \beta\{(1 - G(\hat{c}_{En}(a)))\pi'_{I2m}(a) +$$

(15) $\displaystyle\int_{\underline{c_E}}^{\hat{c}_{En}(a)}(d\pi_{I2d}(a,c_E)/da)g(c_E)dc_E - g(\hat{c}_{En}(a))[\pi_{I2m}(a) - \pi_{I2d}(a,\hat{c}_{En}(a))]\hat{c}'_{En}(a)\}$

When exit is impossible, the incumbent's incentive to increase a will come more from a's

effect on its monopoly profits in period 2 than from its effect on duopoly profits. This

occurs not only because there is less entry when exit is impossible, but also because the

effect on duopoly profits receives greater weight in (14) than (15). This is due to the fact

that the value of duopoly profits in (14), in the exit case, is via entry deterrence, which is

more valuable than the added increment to profit itself. Equation (15), however, has an

added entry deterrence term of its own. From (12), we know that $\hat{c}'_{En}(a) < 0$ if and only

if increases in a reduces the profit of the entrant. Moreover, its magnitude is larger the

more effective a is at reducing the profits of the entrant. Thus, whether an incumbent has

a greater incentive to forego current profits by increasing a when exit is possible than when it isn't will be heavily dependent on how strongly a affects the entrant's profits. If the action a, however, has either no effect on the entrant's profits or increases them (e.g., if it is advertising that expands the market), then it is much more likely that the incumbent will choose a larger a when exit is possible.

Focusing on the case where a is a cost reducing investment, one might also wonder if the threat of entry increases or reduces the incumbent's incentive to reduce costs? In the exit case, one can look at (14) to answer this question. Notice that the marginal benefit from cost reduction, a, can be separated into two different terms:

$$\Pi'_I(a) = \pi'_{I1}(a) + \beta\pi'_{I2m}(a) +$$

(14?)
$$\beta\int_{\underline{c_E}}^{\hat{c}_E(a)}[\frac{d\pi_{I2d}(a,c_E)}{da}\frac{\pi_{I2m}(a)-f}{\pi_{I2d}(a,\hat{c}_E(a))-f} - \pi'_{I2m}(a)]g(c_E)dc_E$$

The first line of the right hand side is the marginal benefit from a when there is no threat of entry. The second line is adjustment in the marginal benefit due to the threat of entry. The threat of entry will increase the incumbent's incentive to reduce costs, when exit is possible, if and only if the second line of (14?) is positive.

One can perform the same decomposition of the marginal incentive to reduce costs when exit is not possible:

$$\Pi'_I(a) = \pi'_{I1}(a) + \beta\pi'_{I2m}(a) +$$

(15?)
$$\beta\int_{\underline{c_E}}^{\hat{c}_{En}(a)}\{\frac{d\pi_{I2d}(a,c_E)}{da} - \pi'_{I2m}(a)\}g(c_E)dc_E$$
$$- \beta g(\hat{c}_{En}(a))[\pi_{I2m}(a) - \pi_{I2d}(a,\hat{c}_{En}(a))]\hat{c}'_{En}(a)$$

As before, the threat of entry increases the incumbents incentive to reduce costs, when exit is not possible, if and only if the last two lines of (15?) are, together, positive.

With completely abstract profit functions it is not possible, in either case, to say if the threat of entry increases or decreases cost reduction incentives. When exit is possible, however, Proposition 3 describes a leading case where one can say that the threat of entry always increases cost reduction incentives.

Proposition 3. Say profits in period 2.3 are determined by a one-shot Cournot quantity-setting game. If the reaction functions are downward sloping, then, if exit is possible, the threat of entry strictly increases the incumbent's incentives to reduce costs. This is not necessarily the case when exit is not possible.

Proof. See Appendix.

This result is really driven by Proposition 2. There can be a reduced incentive to reduce costs in a duopoly market vis-à-vis a monopoly one because the incumbent produces less output. However, when exit is possible, the incumbent only cares about cost reduction in a duopoly market to make its threat of not exiting the market more credible. Thus, the benefit from cost reduction in a duopoly market is that by increasing the credibility of the incumbent's threat not to exit, the incumbent is more likely to be a monopolist rather than a duopolist. So when exit is possible, cost reduction benefits still come from the entire monopoly output. Moreover, the benefit is not just the reduced cost but also the larger price the incumbent gets when it is a monopolist rather than a duopolist. As a result, the threat of entry strictly increases the incumbent's incentive to reduce costs.

The above argument does not work for the Bertrand case due to the discontinuity of the effect of costs on profits. A simple example will illustrate how with Bertrand competition the threat of entry could actually reduce the incumbent's incentive for cost reduction, even when exit is possible. Say the distribution of entrant types who enter are concentrated around two points: either the entrant has costs that are above the monopoly price for the incumbent (say entry costs are tiny), at its original cost level, or its costs are far enough below the incumbent's that it isn't profitable for the incumbent to reduce its costs to that level. Notice, the incumbent's duopoly profits at cutoff level for entry are equal to its monopoly profits. So, the weight on the effect of a duopoly profits is just one; the entry deterrence value of cost reduction does not magnify the direct value of cost reduction on duopoly profits since the incumbent is earning monopoly profits as a duopolist. Thus, for the high cost entrant types, the incentive for cost reduction is unaffected by the threat of entry. If the entrant is of the low cost type, however, then the incumbent has no sales after entry, so cost reduction is of no benefit. Thus, the incentive for cost reduction must be strictly greater when there is no threat of entry.

When exit is not possible, the threat of entry can also either increase or decrease the incumbent's cost reduction incentives, even under Cournot competition. The reason is that, when there is no exit, the entry deterrence benefit from cost reduction is (as Proposition 2 demonstrates) completely independent of the duopoly benefit from cost reduction. Thus, if the entry deterrence benefit is small (either because cost reduction has a small effect on the entrant's profits or because monopoly and duopoly profits do not differ by much) then it is possible for the threat of entry to decrease the incumbent's incentive to reduce costs.

IV. CONCLUSION

When there are fixed costs that can be avoided by exit, exit will sometimes be the incumbent's ex post profit-maximizing strategy. This paper shows that considering this possibility can significantly alter the ability of entry deterring strategies to credibly deter entry. Thus, analyzing the effectiveness of entry deterrence strategies when exit is never optimal (or when the incumbent can credibly commit not to exit the market) can lead to as faulty conclusions about the effectiveness of entry deterrence strategies when exit is possible as assuming the incumbent can commit to a pricing or output policy. These credibility issues could be particularly important in industries where technology is rapidly advancing, making the risk that an entrant could supplant an incumbent quite large. Even where the exit by the incumbent does not happen immediately, as is depicted in this model, the qualitative effects of the possibility of later exit are likely to be similar, though a precise description of such effects is left for future research.

APPENDIX

Proof of Proposition 1. (a) Using (3), (4a?) can be written as follows (where r_p is the probability the high cost incumbent chooses the pooling action):

(A1)
$$\frac{qr_p}{qr_p + (1-q)}\pi_{E2m} + \frac{1-q}{qr_p + (1-q)}\pi_{E2dL} - f_E \leq 0$$

When exit isn't possible, the analogous condition is (here r_{pn} is the probability the high cost incumbent chooses the pooling action when exit is impossible):

(A2)
$$\frac{qr_{pn}}{qr_{pn} + (1-q)}\pi_{E2dH} + \frac{1-q}{qr_{pn} + (1-q)}\pi_{E2dL} - f_E \leq 0$$

If (A2) holds strictly, then a_P must be a complete pooling equilibrium when exit is possible. Otherwise, there would be no entry when exit is impossible, making the pooling option is strictly better when exit is impossible than when it is possible. But the myopically optimal action, a_H, is strictly worse without exit. Thus, if the incumbent is indifferent between the two actions when exit is possible, it will always choose the pooling option when exit is impossible. This ensures that $r_{pn} = 1$. Since Proposition 1 assumes there is no complete pooling equilibrium when exit is possible, $r_p < 1 = r_{pn}$.

Now I consider the case where (A2) holds at equality. Solving for r_{pn} yields:

(A3)
$$r_{pn} = \frac{(1-q)(f_E - \pi_{E2dL})}{q(\pi_{E2dH} - f_E)}$$

Solving (A1) for r_p gives the following:

(A4)
$$r_p \leq \frac{(1-q)(f_E - \pi_{E2dL})}{q(\pi_{E2m} - f_E)}$$

Since monopoly profits are greater than duopoly profits, $r_p < r_{pn}$.

(b) When a_P is not a complete pooling equilibrium when exit is impossible then (A2) holds at equality, by the argument in (a). Since a_P is not a complete pooling equilibrium, the high cost incumbent must be indifferent between a_P and a_H. That is:

(A5)
$$\pi_I(a_P, c_H) = \pi_I(a_H, c_H)$$

When exit is possible entry always follows a_H and the high type always exits following entry. Thus, (A5) becomes:

(A6)
$$\pi_{I1}(a_P, c_H) - f + \beta\{(1 - p_e(a_P))(\pi_{I2m}(c_H) - f)\} = \pi_{I1}(a_H, c_H) - f$$

Solving for the probability of entry after observing a_P gives the following:

(A7)
$$p_e(a_P) = 1 - \frac{\pi_{I1}(a_H, c_H) - \pi_{I1}(a_P, c_H)}{\beta(\pi_{I2m}(c_H) - f)}$$

If exit is not possible, I can write (A5) as follows.

(A8)
$$\pi_{I1}(a_P, c_H) - f + \beta\{p_{en}(a_P)(\pi_{I2d}(c_H) - f) + (1 - p_{en}(a_P))(\pi_{I2m}(c_H) - f)\}$$
$$= \pi_{I1}(a_H, c_H) - f + \beta(\pi_{I2d}(c_H) - f)$$

Now $p_{en}(a_P)$ represents the entry probability with no exit. Solving (A8) for $p_{en}(a_P)$ gives the following.

31

(A7)
$$p_{en}(a_P) = 1 - \frac{\pi_{I1}(a_H, c_H) - \pi_{I1}(a_P, c_H)}{\beta(\pi_{I2m}(c_H) - \pi_{I2d}(c_H))}$$

Since $\pi_{I2m}(c_H) > f > \pi_{I2d}(c_H)$, $p_{en}(a_P) > p_e(a_P)$.

(c) There are two cases to consider, where the pooling action in the exit case deters entry completely and when it doesn't. The former, case (i), occurs if and only if $\beta(\pi_{I2m}(c_H) - f) = \pi_{I1}(a_H, c_H) - \pi_{I1}(a_P, c_H)$. Otherwise, in case (ii), $\beta(\pi_{I2m}(c_H) - f) > \pi_{I1}(a_H, c_H) - \pi_{I1}(a_P, c_H)$, so there is some entry.

Case (i). The total probability of entry in the exit case is $q(1 - r_p)$, since there is only entry when the incumbent has high costs and doesn't pool. The total probability of entry in the no exit case is: $p_{en}(a_P)(1 - q + qr_{pn}) + q(1 - r_{pn})$. Using the equations above, subtracting the probability of entry in the no exit case from the probability of entry in the exit case is at least the following:

(A8)
$$\frac{(1-q)}{\beta\{\pi_{I2m}(c_H) - \pi_{I2d}(c_H))(\pi_{E2dH} - f_E)(\pi_{E2m} - f_E)\}}$$
$$\{(\pi_{E2dH} - \pi_{E2dL})(\pi_{E2m} - f_E)(\pi_{I1}(a_H, c_H) - \pi_{I1}(a_P, c_H))$$
$$- \beta(\pi_{E2dH} - f_E)(\pi_{E2m} - \pi_{E2dL})\{\pi_{I2m}(c_H) - \pi_{I2d}(c_H))\}$$

The likelihood of entry in the exit case less the likelihood in the no exit case exceeds (A8) because (A8) uses the value of r_p from the right hand side of (A4). Now using the fact that $\beta(\pi_{I2m}(c_H) - f) = \pi_{I1}(a_H, c_H) - \pi_{I1}(a_P, c_H)$, I can rewrite this as follows:

(A9)
$$\frac{(1-q)}{\{\pi_{I2m}(c_H) - \pi_{I2d}(c_H))(\pi_{E2dH} - f_E)(\pi_{E2m} - f_E)\}}$$
$$\{(\pi_{E2dH} - \pi_{E2dL})(\pi_{E2m} - f_E)(\pi_{I2m}(c_H) - f)$$
$$- (\pi_{E2dH} - f_E)(\pi_{E2m} - \pi_{E2dL})(\pi_{I2m}(c_H) - \pi_{I2d}(c_H))\}$$

The denominator is positive since monopoly profits exceed duopoly profits and the entrant makes net profits both as a monopolist and when the incumbent's costs are high as a duopolist. The numerator will be positive when c_H is low enough that the entrant gets almost no profits from entry, $(\pi_{E2dH} - f_E) \to 0$, or the high cost incumbent would almost breaks even competing as a duopolist, $\pi_{I2d}(c_H) \to f$. The numerator will be negative when c_H gets so high that the entrant's profit as a duopolist is almost as large as its profit as a monopolist, $\pi_{E2dH} \to \pi_{E2m}$.

Now it only must be shown that the numerator is monotonically decreasing in c_H. Differentiating the numerator of (A9), ignoring the 1-q term, gives the following:

(A10)
$$(\pi_{E2dH} - \pi_{E2dL})(\pi_{E2m} - f_E)\pi'_{I2m}(c_H) -$$
$$(\pi_{E2dH} - f_E)(\pi_{E2m} - \pi_{E2dL})\{\pi'_{I2m}(c_H) - \pi'_{I2d}(c_H)) +$$
$$[(\pi_{E2m} - f_E)\{\pi_{I2m}(c_H) - f) - (\pi_{I2m}(c_H) - \pi_{I2d}(c_H))(\pi_{E2m} - \pi_{E2dL})]\frac{d\pi_{E2dH}}{dc_H}$$

Rearranging terms:

$$(\pi_{E2m} - \pi_{E2dH})(f_E - \pi_{E2dL})\pi'_{I2m}(c_H) +$$

(A11)
$$(\pi_{E2dH} - f_E)(\pi_{E2m} - \pi_{E2dL})\pi'_{I2d}(c_H) +$$

$$[(\pi_{E2m} - f_E)\{\pi_{I2m}(c_H) - f) - (\pi_{I2m}(c_H) - \pi_{I2d}(c_H))(\pi_{E2m} - \pi_{E2dL})]\frac{d\pi_{E2dH}}{dc_H}$$

The first line is negative since E makes more profit as a monopolist than a duopolist, E would lose money entering when I's costs are low, and I's profit is decreasing in its costs. The second line is negative because E makes positive net profit as a duopolist against a high cost I and makes more profit as a monopolist than a duopolist. The third line is negative since $\pi_{I2d}(c_H) < f$, I loses money as a high cost duopolist, $\pi_{E2dL} < f_E$, E loses money as a duopolist with a low cost incumbent, and because E's profits are increasing in I's costs.

Case (ii). The total probability of entry in the exit case is $p_e(a_P)(1 - q + qr_p) + q(1 - r_p)$.

The total probability of entry in the no exit case is: $p_{en}(a_P)(1 - q + qr_{pn}) + q(1 - r_{pn})$.

Using the equations above, subtracting the probability of entry in the no exit case from the probability of entry in the exit case is the following:

$$\frac{(1 - q)(\pi_{I1}(a_H, c_H) - \pi_{I1}(a_P, c_H))}{\beta\{\pi_{I2m}(c_H) - \pi_{I2d}(c_H))\{\pi_{I2m}(c_H) - f)(\pi_{E2dH} - f_E)(\pi_{E2m} - f_E)\}}$$

(A12)
$$\{(f_E - \pi_{E2dL})(\pi_{E2m} - \pi_{E2dH})(\pi_{I2m}(c_H) - \pi_{I2d}(c_H))$$

$$- (\pi_{E2dH} - \pi_{E2dL})(\pi_{E2m} - f_E)(f - \pi_{I2d}(c_H))\}$$

The denominator is positive since monopoly profits exceed both fixed costs and duopoly profits and the entrant makes net profits both as a monopolist and when the incumbent's costs are high as a duopolist. The numerator will be positive when c_H is low enough that the entrant gets almost no profits from entry, $(\pi_{E2dH} - f_E) \to 0$, or the high cost incumbent would almost breaks even competing as a duopolist, $\pi_{I2d}(c_H) \to f$. The numerator will be negative when c_H gets so high that the entrant's profit as a duopolist is almost as large as its profit as a monopolist, $\pi_{E2dH} \to \pi_{E2m}$. Now I show that the numerator term in curly brackets is monotonically decreasing in c_H. Differentiating it gives the following:

$$-[(f - \pi_{I2d}(c_H))(\pi_{E2m} - f_E) + (f_E - \pi_{E2dL})(\pi_{I2m}(c_H) - \pi_{I2d}(c_H))]\frac{d\pi_{E2dH}}{dc_H}$$

(A13)
$$- (f_E - \pi_{E2dL})(\pi_{E2m} - \pi_{E2dH})\{\pi'_{I2m}(c_H) - \pi'_{I2d}(c_H))$$

$$- (\pi_{E2dH} - \pi_{E2dL})(\pi_{E2m} - f_E)\pi'_{I2d}(c_H)$$

Rearranging terms:

$$-[(f - \pi_{I2d}(c_H))(\pi_{E2m} - f_E) + (f_E - \pi_{E2dL})(\pi_{I2m}(c_H) - \pi_{I2d}(c_H))]\frac{d\pi_{E2dH}}{dc_H}$$

(A14)
$$- (f_E - \pi_{E2dL})(\pi_{E2m} - \pi_{E2dH})\pi'_{I2m}(c_H)$$

$$- (\pi_{E2dH} - f_E)(\pi_{E2m} - \pi_{E2dL})\pi'_{I2d}(c_H)$$

Each line in (A14) is clearly negative because of the assumptions on the profit relations. Q.E.D.

Proof of Proposition 3. From equation (14?), it is easy to see that to show that the threat of entry increases the incumbent's incentive to reduce costs it is enough to show that :

(A15)
$$\frac{d\pi_{I2d}(a,c_E)}{da}\frac{\pi_{I2m}(a)-f}{\pi_{I2d}(a,\hat{c}_E(a))-f}-\pi'_{I2m}(a)>0, \forall c_E \in [\underline{c}_E,\hat{c}_E(a)]$$

When the incumbent is a monopolist or a duopolist competing with the highest cost entrant, its gross profits will exceed its fixed operating cost, f. Moreover, the monopoly profit will always exceed the duopoly profit. Thus, if the following is positive then (A15) will be positive:

(A16)
$$\frac{d\pi_{I2d}(a,c_E)}{da}\frac{\pi_{I2m}(a)}{\pi_{I2d}(a,\hat{c}_E(a))}-\pi'_{I2m}(a)>0, \forall c_E \in [\underline{c}_E,\hat{c}_E(a)]$$

Now I use the fact that duopoly profits are determined by a one-shot Cournot quantity setting game. Without loss of generality, I will say that the cost reducing investment is measured in the amount by which costs are reduced. Hence, the incumbent's costs in period 2 are c-a. Thus, the left hand side of (A16) can be written as follows:

(A17)
$$\frac{q_{Id}(4p'_{Id}+(q_{Id}+2q_{Ed})p''_{Id})}{3p'_{Id}+(q_{Id}+q_{Ed})p''_{Id}}\frac{q_{Im}(p_{Im}-(c-a))}{q_{Id}(p_{Id}-(c-a))}-q_{Im}$$

The arguments are suppressed in the above expression. All price terms and their derivatives are functions of the total quantity produced. Expression (A17) is positive if and only if the following inequality holds:

(A18)
$$(1+\frac{(p'_{Id}+q_{Ed}p''_{Id})}{3p'_{Id}+(q_{Id}+q_{Ed})p''_{Id}})\frac{(p_{Im}-(c-a))}{(p_{Id}-(c-a))}>1$$

The second fraction on the left hand side is greater than one since prices in a monopoly are higher than in a duopoly. Thus, (A18) will hold if $\frac{(p'_{Id}+q_{Ed}p''_{Id})}{3p'_{Id}+(q_{Id}+q_{Ed})p''_{Id}}>0$. But this is always positive since the numerator and denominator are both negative by the assumption that the reaction functions are downward sloping.

To show that if exit is not possible the threat of entry can either increase or decrease the incumbent's incentive for cost reduction, under Cournot competition, consider a linear inverse demand function an a uniform distribution of entrant types. That is, let $p(q)=z_1-z_2q$ and let $c_E \sim U(c_{EL},c_{EH})$. The assumption of Cournout competition with these functional forms gives the following explicit forms for the profit functions:

(A19)
$$\pi_{I2d}(a,c_E)=\frac{(z_1-(2(c-a)-c_E))^2}{9z_2};\pi_{I2m}(c_E)=\frac{(z_1-(c-a))^2}{4z_2}$$

$$\pi_{E2d}(a,c_E)=\frac{(z_1-(2c_E-(c-a)))^2}{9z_2};\pi_{E2m}(c_E)=\frac{(z_1-c_E)^2}{4z_2}$$

Using these profit functions and solving (11) for $\hat{c}_{En}(a)$ gives the following:

(A20)
$$\hat{c}_{En}(a)=\frac{1}{2}(c-a+z_1-3\sqrt{f_Ez_2})$$

Using (A19) and (A20), I can write the last two lines of (15?), the added marginal benefit of cost reduction due to the threat of entry, as follows:

(A21)
$$\frac{\beta\{27 f_E z_2 + 2(z_1 + (c-a) - 2c_{EL})(z_1 - 5(c-a) + 4c_{EL})\}}{72 z_2 (c_{EH} - c_{EL})}$$

Expression (A21) is positive if and only if:

(A22)
$$\frac{1}{5}\{5c - 7c_{EL} + 2z_1 - 3\sqrt{(z_1 - c_{EL})^2 + \frac{15 f_E z_2}{2}}\} < a$$
$$< \frac{1}{5}\{5c - 7c_{EL} + 2z_1 + 3\sqrt{(z_1 - c_{EL})^2 + \frac{15 f_E z_2}{2}}\}$$

Thus, when exit is not possible, with these functional forms, the threat of entry will decrease the incumbent's incentive to reduce costs when the optimal amount of cost reduction is either very large or very small. This will more likely be the case when the first period loss of profit from cost reduction is very small or very large. For example, when the parameters take on the following values:

$$c = 3.5, c_{EL} = 0, c_{EH} = 7, z_1 = 5, z_2 = 1, f_E = 1, \beta = .95$$

the threat of entry reduces the incumbent's incentive to reduce costs when the first period loss from cost reduction is $-a^2$, but increases the incumbent's incentive to reduce costs when this loss is given by $-.4a^2$. Q.E.D.

REFERENCES

Albaek, Svend and Overgaard, Per Baltzer. "Advertising and Pricing to Deter or Accommodate Entry when Demand is Unknown: Comment." *The International Journal of Industrial Organization*, March 1994, 12(1), pp.83-87.

Arvan, Lanny. "Sunk Capacity Costs, Long-Run Fixed Costs, and Entry Deterrence under Complete and Incomplete Information." *Rand Journal of Economics*, Spring 1986, 17(1), pp.105-21.

Bagwell, Kyle. "A Model of Competitive Limit Pricing." *Journal of Economics and Management Strategy*, Winter 1992, 1(4), pp. 585-606.

_____ and Ramey, Garey. "Advertising and Limit Pricing." *Rand Journal of Economics*, Spring 1988, 19(1), pp.59-71.

_____. "Advertising and Pricing to Deter or Accommodate Entry when Demand is Unknown." *The International Journal of Industrial Organization*, March 1990, 8(1), pp. 93-113.

_____. "Oligopoly Limit Pricing." *Rand Journal of Economics*, Summer 1991, 22(2), pp.155-72

_____. "Capacity, Entry, and Forward Induction." *Rand Journal of Economics*, Winter 1996, 27(4), pp.660-80.

Benoit, Jean-Pierre and Krishna, Vijay. "Entry Deterrence and Dynamic Competition." *The International Journal of Industrial Organization*, 1991, 9(4), pp.477-95.

Bulow, Jeremy; Geanakoplos, John and Klemperer, Paul. "Holding Idle Capacity to Deter Entry." *The Economic Journal*, March 1985, 95, pp.178-82.

Dixit, Avinash. "The Role of Investment in Entry-Deterrence." *The Economic Journal*, March 1980, 90, pp.95-106.

Eaton, B. Curtis and Lindsey, Richard G. "Exit Barriers are Entry Barriers: The Durability of Capital as a Barrier to Entry." *The Bell Journal of Economics*, Autumn 1980, 11(2), pp.721-29.

The Economist, "The New Enforcers." October 7, 2000. http://www.economist.com/business/displayStory.cfm?Story_ID=387757

Harrington, Joseph E. Jr. "Oligopolistic Entry Deterence under Incomplete Information." *Rand Journal of Economics*, Summer 1987, 18(2), pp.211-31

Judd, Kenneth J. "Credible Spatial Preemption." *Rand Journal of Economics*, Summer 1985, 16(2), pp.153-166.

LeBlanc, Greg. "Signalling Strength: Limit Pricing and Predatory Pricing." *Rand Journal of Economics*, Winter 1992, 23(4), pp.493-506.

Martin, Stephen. "Oligopoly Limit Pricing: Strategic Substitutes and Strategic Complements." *The International Journal of Industrial Organization*, March 1995, 13(1), pp.41-65.

Maskin, Eric S. "Uncertainty and Entry Deterrence." *Economic Theory*, August 1999, 14(2), pp.429-37.

Matthews, Steven A. and Mirman, Leonard J. "Equilibrium Limit Pricing: The Effects of Private Information and Stochastic Demand." *Econometrica*, July 1983, 51(4), pp. 981-96.

Milgrom, Paul and Robers, John. "Limit Pricing and Entry under Incomplete Information: An Equilibrium Analysis." *Econometrica*, March 1982, 50(2), pp.443-59.

Nalebuff, Barry. "Credible Pretrial Negotiation." *Rand Journal of Economics*, Summer 1987, 18(2), pp. 198-210.

Salonen, Hannu. "Entry Detrrence and Limit Pricing under Asymmetric Information about Common Costs." *Games and Economic Behavior*, March 1994, 6(2), pp.312-27.

San Jose Mercury News. "American Begins Notifying Workers Which Jobs Will Go." June 24, 1993.

Schmalensee, Richard. "Advertising and Entry Deterrence: An Exploratory Model." *Journal of Political Economy*, August 1983, 91(4), pp.636-53.

Spence, Michael. "Entry, Investment, and Oligopolistic Pricing." *Bell Journal of Economics*, Autumn 1977, 8(2), pp.534-44.

Waldman, Michael. "The Simple Case of Entry Deterrence Reconsidered." UCLA Working Paper No. 517, September 1988.

Washington Post. "The Southwest Revolution." September 12, 1993.

www.ingramcontent.com/pod-product-compliance
Lightning Source LLC
Chambersburg PA
CBHW081243170526
45165CB00009B/3171